33 PRAYERS
For Your Future
HUSBAND

SCHUYLER ELLIOT

33 Prayers For Your Future Husband

Preparing Your Heart and Fighting In Prayer On His Behalf

Written by Schuyler Elliot

Copyright © 2024 Schuyler Elliot, LLC

ISBN: 979-8-218-37057-2

www.schuylerelliot.com

ACKNOWLEDGEMENT

The power of prayer was introduced to me at a very young age. I remember walking up the long hall and cracking open the door to my parent's room after my father had already left for work. I would hear my mother's worship music blasting and the sound of her voice praying as she cleaned and got herself ready for the day. Then, I would walk into her room and sit on her floor as I watched her joyful spirit lift her hands and close her eyes while she gave thanks to her Lord. I loved watching her; I felt such a peace while being in the room as she prepared for her day while covering her family in prayer.

Little did she know back then that those were seeds that were being planted in that little girl lying on the cozy carpet of her mother's master bedroom. Little did she know that that little girl was looking up to her, admiring how she never failed to uplift her husband and children before the Lord as soon as she woke up in the morning. Little did she know that she was being watched, observed, and studied. The way she prayed, how she prayed, and what she prayed for were all tools that she was placing in that little girl's arsenal that she would one day need.

I remember watching my mother fix breakfast for my brother and I while holding the house phone on speaker in one hand and a spatula in the other. She would pray with my father on the phone every morning as he drove to work. As a kid, this routine seemed ordinary to me, just like when my mother would smile at me through the rearview mirror on the way to school and say, "Alright, you guys, it's time to pray!" My brother and I would, at times, sigh because we knew her prayers were always powerful but sometimes a bit lengthy. Back then, I just thought of it as mom being mom, but I now know that was her being the prayer warrior God created her to be.

My mother was a fighter. She prayed for her family and knew that the enemy was after us. Every day, she covered each one of us with the blood of Jesus, and I am intensely grateful for her faithfulness. She never hesitated to tell my brother and I where her help came from, and she always boasted in her Lord and Savior. My mother was a disciple of Jesus Christ who made two more disciples of Jesus Christ, my brother and I. She made our home a house of prayer, praise, and worship. I owe her everything because she taught me how to fight in prayer, how to kneel before God, and how to become a woman after God's heart. It is because of her, yes, that you are even reading this book right now at this moment. I now understand that those early mornings and long car rides of prayer and worship were not for fun but for waging war against the enemy's schemes. She disrupted the plans of the enemy, and I might not have understood that then, but I surely do now.

I remember frequently looking through my grandmother's church notes, prayer journals, and devotionals throughout my childhood. I will never forget the early mornings when my grandmother had her devotions with her cup of coffee, cream, and no sugar.

I will always be grateful to my mother and grandmother, who paved the way for me through their example of prayer and sacrifice. Mom, thank you for teaching me everything, passing on your love and wisdom, and instilling in me the same faith that your mother passed down to you. Your love, guidance, and support have been instrumental in shaping me into the woman I am today.

This is a tribute to the women of faith who showed me the way to my Lord and Savior. I love you both more than words can express. Your legacy will not stop here.

Oh, Grandma, how I wish you could see the fruit of your hard work and faith. I miss you terribly.

In loving memory, LaDonne Mingo. March 1st, 2021.

DEDICATION

Dear future husband,

It's your future wife here. Although I do not even know who you are at this moment, I am dedicating this book to you. In this season of waiting and preparation, I am taking full advantage of preparing myself to become the woman the Lord created me to be and the prayer warrior that you and our future children deserve. This season is crucial for both of us so that we may learn to love, support, and serve each other selflessly to experience a marriage full of love with Christ as our foundation.

Our singleness in this season is a gift so that we may both, separately, prepare to take on this world hand in hand, together with the presence of God leading us wherever we go. My prayer is that you fully step into your purpose and calling with power, strength, authority, and confidence that only comes from reliance on our Savior, Jesus Christ. I also pray that you don't grow weary in your faith, but that through trials and tests, your faith is perfected through Christ.

Before time, God picked you as my partner, my protector, my warrior, my best friend, and most importantly, my husband. I cannot wait to take on life with you, walk down the aisle on our wedding day, and say yes to the man of my dreams, but most importantly, the man of my prayers. I have spent countless hours praying for you and will never stop bathing you and our future children in prayer. Although I am eager to meet you and begin life with you, I am content in patiently waiting, preparing, praying, and working towards becoming the wife that God created me to be. I cannot wait to meet my best friend and partner in crime.

I love you now, always, and forever.

Your future wife,

Schuyler 🩶

CONTENTS

LEADERSHIP IN MARRIAGE

ABOUT THE AUTHOR

Schuyler Elliot, is using her voice and social media influence to reach her generation with a message of hope and truth that a life in Jesus Christ can not only radically transform lives but can change the world. Schuyler is the host of the cutting-edge platform "The Kill Culture Podcast." Through this platform, she spreads the message of Jesus Christ and encourages young adults worldwide to place their trust in God. Schuyler's passion for leading, speaking, and ministering in young adult ministry shows her commitment to pointing this generation to the cross despite the opinions of an ever-opposing culture. Her mission is to demonstrate that a life fully devoted to Christ holds more value and power than the cultural norms of today's society.

In addition to her work in ministry, Schuyler's dedication to the fashion and modeling industry is also a testament to her commitment to bridging the gap between the two worlds. Schuyler's mission is to continue demonstrating that Christians can not only be on fire for Christ but can also have fun, thrive, create, and represent Him in the fashion and entertainment industry.

Her story is one of inspiration and motivation for young adults worldwide. Contact Schuyler Elliot for speaking engagements or other events

www.schuylerelliot.com

SOCIAL MEDIA

INTRODUCTION

Hello there! I am so excited that you decided to take this step in committing to praying for your future husband. As women, we often spend our time discussing everything we would like in a husband without taking the time to pray that he grows into the man that God created him to be. As women, it is crucial that we learn to pray for our future spouses, even if we haven't met them yet. While it's great to think about our hopes, dreams, and wishes, we must also learn to fight for them through prayer. Your spouse is out there, somewhere in the world, living life and fighting the same struggles and battles that you are. So, as much as you want to dream about what kind of person he is, it is more important to go to war on his behalf so that he can become the fully surrendered man of God this world needs him to be.

You aren't waiting for a spouse; you have one. It's just not your season to be married to them yet, and that is okay. There is so much beauty in the waiting season because it's a season of preparation and maturation, which will only make your marriage sweeter and worth the wait. Or in some cases, maybe you are dating them but have yet to be married to them. Use this time wisely! Take this season to use the power of prayer and begin praying for your life partner in detail.

I wrote this book to encourage you that your waiting season does not have to be unproductive; this season is valuable and necessary for you and your future spouse. In this book, you will find detailed, crafted prayers that I have personally written to cover my future husband in the power of prayer. Although I do not know who he is yet, I am trusting God's timing! Being in a season of waiting and prayer will build a firm foundation set on Christ before marriage is even in the equation. I pray that this book empowers you to go to God with your desires while staying rooted in the power of prayer!

Psalm 27:14 states,
"Wait for the Lord; be strong and take heart."

THE POWER OF A PRAYING WOMAN

Ladies, are you ready to tap into the power of prayer and see God do amazing things in and through your future marriage? Let me tell you, things change when you use the power of prayer to make things happen!

Matthew 21:22 says, "And whatever you ask in prayer, you will receive, if you have faith."

Did you know that couples who pray together have an incredibly high success rate of staying together? Yes, you heard that right! Let's look at some statistics for a quick second. 50% of marriages end in divorce. Now, that's a downer to hear, but let me tell you this next stat that will blow your mind. Did you know that couples who pray together have an incredibly low divorce rate of only 1 in 1,500 marriages? Wow! So basically, couples who pray together stay together! God wants you to have a healthy and beautiful marriage! Why? Because He is the One who created love and marriage in the first place!

By putting God at the center of your marriage, you're setting yourself up for a healthy and fulfilling relationship. After all, God is the Creator of love and marriage, and He wants nothing more than to see His sons and daughters thrive in union!

So, if we have full access to the power of prayer right now, why would we wait until marriage to use that tool? When you pray, it pulls the power of God right down to the situation you are praying for. Praying for your future partner is an excellent tool to invite God's power into your life and his, creating a strong foundation for a healthy and successful marriage.

Begin creating a habit of praying for your future spouse today so that God can move in power in both of your lives, making you both the healthiest versions of yourselves before the wedding bells ring. By praying together, you are inviting God's goodness and blessings into your relationship, making it stronger and more fulfilling than you ever thought it could be.

Your season as newlyweds is not the time to heal from past trauma or to finally let go of toxic ways. Your season as newlyweds is the time to build your forever on a strong and healthy foundation with the partner God has hand-picked for you! Prepare, fix, heal, and let God mold your heart now so that in marriage, you and your husband can start the right way, the way that the Lord desires you to begin: ready, healthy, and confident!

Proverbs 18:21 ESV "Death and life are in the power of the tongue, and those who love it will eat its fruits."

The prayers that you will find in this book are powerful, but only if you use your words to speak them out loud. The Word says, *"Death and life are in the power of the tongue"* which means you hold the power to speak life into your future husband and marriage; what a great opportunity! Declare healing and wholeness over your future husband and marriage, starting today!

Welcome to your journey of beginning "33 Prayers for Your Future Husband."

Let's get started today, shall we?

SECTION

One

HEART
HEALTH

Philippians 1:6 ESV
*"And I am sure of this,
that He who began a good
work in you will bring it to
completion at the
day of Jesus Christ."*

In this first section of the *33 Prayers for Your Future Husband* book, you will be placing an emphasis on praying for your future husband's heart posture while also doing a double check on yours; why is that important? Here, let me show you.

> *Luke 6:45 ESV states, "The good person out of the good treasure of his heart produces good, and the evil person out of his evil treasure produces evil, for out of the abundance of the heart his mouth speaks."*

It is crucial to prioritize our heart health because it impacts every aspect of our lives. Our thoughts, feelings, and actions all stem from the condition of our hearts. While one may claim to have a relationship with God, a relationship with Christ can only be achieved through a sincere transformation of the heart. Our goal should be to strive for a healthy and clean heart so that the Holy Spirit can move in and through us!

> *Proverbs 4:23 ESV "Keep your heart with all vigilance, for from it flow the springs of life."*

So, how do we truly focus on our heart health? We work to mold our hearts to the Word of God so that our hearts begin to look like His. The more we chase our Lord, the more His desires become our desires, and His reasoning becomes our way of life, so that we may experience the fullness that He desires for us. If you are seeking to have a healthy marriage and healthy relationships in life as a whole, it all comes down to the posture of your heart.

So, as you're praying these prayers for your future husband, pray and ask the Lord to reveal areas of your heart that need changing. Is it your vanity? Comparison? Past trauma? Spirit of Fatherlessness? Fear of the future? Past hurt in relationships? Anything that hinders you from moving forward in life and your relationship with Christ is a sign of a heart that is in need of some healing. And if that's you today, that is okay! Our Lord is a Healer and He is just itching to heal you and show you a better way to live! We can receive healing in our hearts by asking God to come in and reveal and heal the areas of our hearts that need mending.

Jeremiah 33:6: "Behold, I will bring to it health and healing, and I will heal them and reveal to them abundance of prosperity and security."

Psalm 147:3: "He heals the brokenhearted and binds up their wounds."

A PRAYER FOR YOUR JOURNEY

Dear Lord,

I thank You and praise You for chasing after me and pursuing me. Thank You for consuming me with Your love. I declare my dependency on You, Father, for everything in my life. I desire a whole and healed heart to experience a life full of abundance and overflow. I pray and ask Lord that You reveal all areas of my life that need mending and healing. I die to my old ways of life and pursue a new life in You in pursuit of healthy relationships and experiences. Lord, I also pray that You reveal areas of my life that are in need of growth so that I may become mature and complete in You, ready for my purpose and future. I know and declare that You have good plans for my life, so I am asking that You prepare my heart and mind to receive those good plans, in Jesus' name.

I place my identity not in who the world says I am but in who You say I am. I renounce and reject all lies of the enemy that seek to hold me captive in Jesus' name. I free myself from the destructive habits and cycles that are from the enemy in Jesus' name. I invite You into every area of my life, and I pray for healing in areas that are keeping me from my future. I speak healing over myself in Jesus' name. I renounce and break off every generational curse that is attached to my bloodline in the mighty name of Jesus Christ. I declare and claim my freedom in You, Lord. Make me a new creation in You, Father. I receive the authority that You have given me in the name of Jesus. Thank You for being a Healer, Lord. Holy Spirit, I pray that as I begin this journey of praying for my future husband, You will not only touch my husband's life but my own.

In Jesus' name, I pray, amen.

PRAYER #1

HIS HEART

Matthew 22:37 ESV; Proverbs 23:26 NIV

Matthew 22:37 ESV "You shall love the Lord your God with all your heart and with all your soul and with all your mind."

Dear Lord,

I pray for my future spouse and that his heart is for You first. I pray that You will lead, grow, and mature him through Your Word. I pray that he loves You above all else and continues to chase You and Your will for his life. Lord, fill him with an abundance of wisdom and give him a strong spirit of discernment as he leads us in marriage. I pray for protection over his heart and mind in Jesus' name. I pray that he will guard his heart and guard my heart as his wife. Father, I pray that You perfect my husband's willpower, and when temptation arises, give him the strength and discipline to take the way out and not give into temptation. Lord, I pray that You heal his heart from anything he has faced in his past and anything that he is facing right now. I pray that my future husband will depend on You for anything and everything in his life.

Proverbs 23:26 NIV *"My son, give Me your heart and let your eyes delight in My ways"*

Lord, I pray that my future husband has a strong and intimate relationship with You and that he learns to clearly understand who You are and how You are moving in his life. Reveal Your purpose for his life to him, Lord, and show him what his mission in life is. I pray that my future husband will be sensitive to the Holy Spirit and allow himself to be led by You, Father. I pray that he continues to draw near to You while he works to remove any distractions in his life that keep him from hearing Your voice clearly. Remove any darkness from his heart in Jesus' name and purify his heart with the blood of Jesus Christ so that Your power will be evident in his life.

Give him the humility to surrender his future to You Lord; I pray he will trust You even when he doesn't understand. Give him a heart after You and a heart to serve You and

Your Kingdom. I pray that he will constantly work to make his heart look more like Yours each and every day. Lord, I pray that he will reflect Your character and strive to love people the way You love them. I pray that he is willing to acknowledge and handle his emotions and doesn't push them away. Lord, I pray that he will run to You when his heart is feeling heavy and that he will cast his worries on You.

In Jesus' name, I pray, Amen.

PRAYER #2

UNDERSTANDING HIS PURPOSE

1 Peter 2:9 NIV; Proverbs 19:21 NIV; Matthew 28:19-20 ESV; Psalm 138:8 ESV

1 Peter 2:9 "But you are a chosen people, a royal priesthood, a holy nation, God's special possession, that you may declare the praises of Him who called you out of darkness into His wonderful light."

Dear Lord,

Thank You for today. I thank You for guiding my husband through every season of his life. I thank You for creating him for a specific purpose and mission in this world. I pray that You reveal Your purpose for his life to him and that he will be dedicated to fulfilling the call on his life for Your glory. Father, show him daily that You created him on purpose for a specific purpose. I pray that my future husband is talented in many distinct skills and abilities, and I pray that You give him patience and a teachable spirit while he learns new crafts, skills, and lessons. I pray that You sharpen his spiritual gifts and give him opportunities to use and master those gifts.

Father, I pray that he will desperately depend on You for anything and everything. I pray that he will exercise the authority You have given him with responsibility and honor. Lord, I pray that he will include me as his wife in every area of his mission, calling, and ministry. I pray that my husband and I will be unified in our decision making and trust in Your instruction together as husband and wife. Give him the humility to submit to You first and rely on You for strength in every area of his life. Show him how to lead in his purpose with passion, vision, authority, patience, and love. If he is unsure about his purpose, Lord, I pray that he will seek You even when he is uncertain.

I also pray, Lord, that he will be hopeful about our marriage and understand the specific purpose of our marriage in the Kingdom of God. I command any feelings of unworthiness to go from him now in the name of Jesus Christ. I come against any feelings of inadequacy and insecurity in Jesus' name. I command the spirit of pride to depart from him now in the name of Jesus and by the power of the blood of the Lamb. Lord, give him the spiritual maturity to handle his calling with honor and respect. In the name of Jesus, I come against any spirit that is telling him that he is not worthy or that he is incapable of completing the mission You are calling him to complete. Lord, I pray that You equip and prepare him for his purpose. Help him to remember that his strength comes from You alone.

In Jesus' name, Amen.

PRAYER #3

COMMUNICATION

James 1:19 ESV; Proverbs 15:1 ESV; Colossians 4:6 ESV

Colossians 4:6 ESV "Let your speech always be gracious, seasoned with salt, so that you may know how you ought to answer each person."

Dear Heavenly Father,

I come before You, thanking and praising You for my husband. I pray that he will have an unbreakable bond with You. I pray that his communication with You will grow stronger and stronger every day. I pray that he will learn how to discern Your voice from his own thoughts so that he can clearly hear Your instructions. I pray that when facing trials, he will seek Your voice even more. I pray that the foundation of my relationship with my husband will be rooted in communicating in love and patience with each other. I pray that my future husband will learn to have the spiritual maturity to express his thoughts and feelings to me as his wife.

James 1:19 ESV *"let every person be quick to hear, slow to speak, slow to anger"*

Lord, I pray that my husband and I will provide a safe environment for each other to express our feelings and emotions within our marriage. Give us a strong, intimate, and emotional bond with each other on the foundation of communication. Grow us both, Father, to learn how to communicate effectively, seeking to understand each other. Give my husband and I patience with each other as we communicate and have tough conversations within our marriage. I pray that within our marriage, my husband and I will be quick to listen, slow to speak, and slow to get angry. Father, I pray that even in the heat of an argument, my husband and I will always communicate in love and remember that we are not each other's enemy.

God, give my husband and I power in our words to uplift and build each other up. I pray that we will always use our words to encourage and reassure each other in our marriage. I pray that my husband and I will always communicate with each other first before we involve external counseling. I pray that my husband and I will be loyal to each other in every way imaginable as we work to keep our marriage personal and intimate. Bless our communication skills as husband and wife,

In Jesus' name, Amen!

PRAYER #4

HIS FAMILY

Genesis 2:24 ESV; Ephesians 6:2 ESV; Exodus 20:12 ESV

Exodus 20:12 ESV "Honor your father and your mother, that your days may be long in the land that the Lord your God is giving you."

In the name of Jesus,

I come before You, uplifting my future husband's family. I pray that he has a strong and close relationship with his family. I pray that his family loves You and puts You first as the Lord and Savior of their lives. If his family does not know You, Lord, I declare they will come to know You and serve You with a submitted heart. I pray that my husband honors his parents in every situation and treats them with respect and love, no matter the circumstance. Lord, allow our marriage to exemplify God's guidance, provision, and love. I pray he is kind, caring, and compassionate towards his family. Father, I pray that my husband honors his parents but will prioritize our marriage above his family when the time comes. I pray that You give him the wisdom and strength to set healthy boundaries with his family. I come against any division within his family in Jesus' name.

Genesis 2:24 ESV *"Therefore a man shall leave his father and his mother and hold fast to his wife, and they shall become one flesh."*

Father, I pray that he learns how to be a man of God and a good husband from his father's example. If he doesn't have a good relationship with his father or if he has lost his father, I pray that You will bring along a strong, godly example of a husband and father for my future husband to learn from. If he does not have a strong relationship with his family, I pray he will find his comfort and identity in You alone. I also pray my husband's family will love and accept me in their family with excitement and open arms. I pray that they will accept me as one of their own and support me and my husband's marriage and family. Bless my husband's relationship with his family members.

In Jesus' name, I pray, Amen.

PRAYER #5

HIS MIND

**Philippians 4:8 ESV; Romans 12:2 ESV; Isaiah 26:3 ESV;
Ephesians 4:22-24 ESV; Colossians 3:1-2 ESV**

*Philippians 4:8 ESV "Finally, brothers, whatever
is true, whatever is honorable, whatever is just,
whatever is pure, whatever is lovely, whatever is
commendable, if there is any excellence, if there is
anything worthy of praise, think about these things."*

Dear Heavenly Father,

I pray for supernatural protection for my husband's mind. Lord, guard his mind all the days of his life. I pray that You will give my husband the strength and power to resist and walk away from temptation. You always provide a way out of temptation; I pray that my husband will be able to identify the attack quickly and have the discipline and strength to take the way out. I pray he has a close relationship with You and will continue to hear Your voice in every season of his life. I pray that You transform him into a mighty powerhouse man of God who is constantly chasing after You and putting You first in his life. I pray that he will continuously work to renew his mind through Your Word and Your instruction. Father, give him a teachable spirit that allows You to constantly renew his mind through Your Word daily. If any areas of his life and character need to be transformed, I pray that he will desire growth and fully surrender to You so he can become the man You have called him to be. I pray for supernatural protection over his mind through the blood of Jesus Christ.

Romans 12:2 ESV *"Do not be conformed to this world, but be transformed by the renewal of your mind, that by testing you may discern what is the will of God, what is good and acceptable and perfect."*

Father, bless him with an abundance of wisdom that comes from You alone. I pray that You secure him in Your confidence and help him always remember who he is in You. I command any mental illness and disease to go in Jesus' name, by the power of the blood of Jesus Christ! I pray that You show him how to focus his mind on You even when distractions come his way. Remove any and all distractions from his life that are keeping him from You, in Jesus' name. I pray that he will keep his mind locked on You and not get distracted by the traps of the enemy.

Father, give him the discernment to identify any Jezebels that may come across his path and give him the spiritual maturity to walk away. I pray that You allow him to grow in spiritual maturity as he grows in You, making himself more like you each and everyday. Even when pressure arises, I pray that he will focus his mind on You, looking to you for guidance and peace. May Your Word lead and guide him always.

In Jesus' name, I pray, Amen.

PRAYER #6

DYING TO SELF

Galatians 2:20 NIV; Luke 9:23 ESV; Galatians 5:24 NLT.

Galatians 2:20 NIV "I have been crucified with Christ and I no longer live, but Christ lives in me. The life I now live in the body, I live by faith in the Son of God, who loved me and gave Himself for me."

Dear Heavenly Father,

I come before You, uplifting my husband to You. I pray that my husband will understand who You are and know he cannot do anything without You. I pray he will develop a desperate and strong dependence on You for everything in his life. I pray that my husband pursues You passionately and continues to put You first every day of his life. Holy Spirit, teach him how to love compassionately the way that You love us, through patience and sacrifice. I pray that You give him a fierce and strong heart to protect the Kingdom of God and our marriage at all costs. Teach him to deny himself and crucify his flesh so that he may become a fully surrendered servant.

Luke 9:23 ESV *"If anyone would come after Me, let him deny himself and take up his cross daily and follow Me."*

Lord, I pray that my future husband will know the importance of dying to his flesh so that he may be a clean vessel ready to be used by You. I pray You show him how to deny his flesh of its sinful desires and give him the strength and wisdom to walk away from worldly temptations. I pray that my future husband dies to his ways, picks up his cross, and follows You. Father, I pray that You continue to work in his life and prepare his heart for our marriage and union. Mold him into the strong man of God that You created him to be, Lord. I pray that You prepare his heart to lead our future family and to lead me as his wife.

Father, I pray that You will place a strong desire in his heart to please You in the way he leads me as his wife. I pray that You remove all selfishness and pride from his heart so that he can fully give himself to You and our marriage. I pray that we both deny ourselves to serve each other wholeheartedly in marriage. I pray that my future husband and I will overcome difficult situations in unity with love, patience, and faith. Lord, give my husband and I the strength to persevere in any and all seasons of life.

In Jesus' name, Amen.

PRAYER #7

POWER

**Colossians 1:11 NIV; 1 Corinthians 2:5 NIV;
2 Corinthians 10:3-6 ESV**

*Colossians 1:11 NIV "being strengthened with all
power according to His glorious might so that you
may have great endurance and patience"*

Dear Lord,

I thank You for my husband, and I thank You for the power that we have access to through the blood of Jesus Christ. Father, I come before You, praying that You equip my husband with Your supernatural power in Jesus' name. Guard his heart and mind, Lord. I pray he will have a strong understanding of Your power and what Your power can equip him to do. I also pray that he and I learn to understand the importance of always remaining surrendered to You and Your Word. Lord, prepare him to do Your work without fear, doubt, or hesitation. Father, I pray that You strengthen us with endurance so we may run the race of life with power and authority. I pray that my future husband and I will continue to learn how to access and operate in Your power.

1 Corinthians 2:5 NIV *"so that your faith might not rest on human wisdom, but on God's power."*

Anoint my husband, Father, and sharpen the gifts that You have given him. Lord, I pray that my future husband and I will be a powerhouse couple for the Kingdom of God, fully relying on You. God, I pray that he and I will keep You at the center of our relationship, looking to You for guidance, strength, and wisdom. I pray that Your power will be the foundation of our marriage. Lord, equip us to do Your work together in complete unity, operating as one through Your power, Jesus. I pray that my future husband and I will pick each other up when one of us is not running in full strength. Lord, I pray that he and I will lead each other back to the Word of God, no matter what we are facing in our lives. I speak Jesus over my husband. God, I speak the power of the Holy Spirit over my husband. Holy Spirit, go before us and invade our marriage in Jesus' mighty name. Thank You, Father; we know our strength and power is from You alone.

In Jesus' name, Amen.

PRAYER #8

A HEART OF GENEROSITY

2 Corinthians 9:7 ESV; Acts 20:35 ESV; Luke 6:38 ESV.

2 Corinthians 9:7 ESV "Each one must give as he has decided in his heart, not reluctantly or under compulsion, for God loves a cheerful giver."

Dear Lord,

I thank You for giving me this season of my life to grow closer to You and bathe my future husband and marriage in prayer. Father, I pray that You bless my husband with a selfless heart that chases after You every day of his life. I pray that he has the heart to serve those around him, as You have called us both to do. God, I pray that he is very generous with his time, finances, energy, attention, and patience. Father, I pray that his heart reflects Yours as he grows closer and closer to You. I pray that we both honor You in how we love and care for others. Lord, I pray that You will bless us abundantly so that we may be a blessing to others. I pray that our first and most important ministry will be our marriage because if we are not properly taking care of our marriage, we will fail to do the work that You have called us to do together, as husband and wife.

Acts 20:35 ESV *"In all things I have shown you that by working hard in this way we must help the weak and remember the words of the Lord Jesus, how He himself said, 'It is more blessed to give than to receive."*

Luke 6:38 ESV *"give, and it will be given to you. Good measure, pressed down, shaken together, running over, will be put into your lap. For with the measure you use it will be measured back to you."*

I pray that he and I will have selfless hearts to give and minister to others without hesitation. Father, I pray that You give us the endurance to continue to pour into the lives around us without growing weary. I pray that You work on our hearts to become more generous to those we come in contact with, and I pray that we will practice our generosity toward each other within our marriage. Father, bless him with a heart that's after You and keep him rooted in humility. I also pray that he will always look to You, Jesus, as an example of how he should live his life in love and with perfect patience.

In Jesus' name, Amen.

PRAYER #9

HIS WORDS

Proverbs 18:21 NIV; Proverbs 11:17 TLB; Proverbs 15:1 NLT; Psalm 19:14 ESV

Proverbs 18:21 NIV "The tongue has the power of life and death"

Lord,

I thank You for my future husband, wherever he is right now at this moment. I pray that he is a man of integrity and that those around him admire his faithfulness and honor. I pray that his character is a reflection of Your heart, Father. Cleanse his mouth, Lord, from any speech that is not of You; I pray that his words will uplift and encourage those around him. I come against any negative speech or words of doubt that are keeping him from advancing and moving forward in his life. I pray that he doesn't use his words to crack hurtful jokes or tear others down in any way. I pray that as he grows closer to You, his heart and speech will become more like Yours, Father, and I also pray that the fruit of his relationship with You will be apparent and evident in his life. Convict his heart of any communication that is not of You. I pray that he will know the importance and weight of his words so that he will choose them wisely. Lord, give him the ability to communicate efficiently and effectively with others in a loving and uplifting way.

Proverbs 11:17 TLB *"Your own soul is nourished when you are kind; it is destroyed when you are cruel."*

Proverbs 15:1 NLT *"A gentle answer deflects anger, but harsh words make tempers flare."*

Father, anoint his words with Your power and authority so that when he speaks, people listen and feel the power of God through his words. I pray that You will always give him a desire to communicate, even when tough conversations need to be had. I pray, Father, that he will communicate in love, patience, and spiritual maturity. In our marriage, I pray that my husband and I will have a close and intimate bond because of our ability to communicate clearly, calmly, and lovingly. I pray that my husband will use words to uplift and protect me emotionally and spiritually. I pray that my words will always be comforting and uplifting to my husband in every season of our lives. Lord, give him the knowledge and wisdom to pray aloud and make declarations to You daily. Lord, I pray that he has a strong prayer life and is desperate for constant communication with You. Father, give him love, gentleness, and wisdom in his tongue,

In Jesus' name, Amen.

PRAYER #10

HIS CONFIDENCE

Romans 8:31-39 ESV; 1 John 4:4 NLT

*1 John 4:4 NLT "But you belong to God, my dear
children. You have already won a victory over
those people, because the Spirit who lives in you is
greater than the spirit who lives in the world."*

Father,

I thank You for my husband; I thank You for his life. I uplift my husband to You, asking that You fill him with an abundance of confidence. I pray he has a strong understanding of who he is in You. I pray that he will run to You when he is doubting or feeling insecure. Fill his heart with Your confidence that is rooted in humility and gentleness; and fill him with boldness from the Holy Spirit. I pray that my future husband leans on Your understanding, even in times when he might not understand what You are calling him to do. Give him the strength to trust You in every situation. I pray that his faith will always be combined with his actions. I pray that my husband learns how to trust You now so that he will lead with confidence and faith in our marriage without fear or doubt. I pray that my husband and I will be a bold couple on fire for You, Lord. I pray that he and I will be abundantly confident in Your Word and our relationship with You throughout our marriage.

Romans 8:37 ESV *"We are more than conquerors through Him who loved us."*

Father, I pray that You give my husband Your supernatural strength so that the trials and weight of this world will not crush him but increase his faith and strengthen his heart. I pray that he will rise up in Your power even in times of adversity. God, I pray that my husband will continuously pursue You and chase after all that You have for him. I also pray that my husband will never stop pursuing me in all stages of our relationship and marriage. Father, I pray that my husband will have confidence in our marriage and know that I support him, love him, and will be faithful to him only. I come against the spirit of deceit from the enemy in Jesus name. Lord, give my husband supernatural discernment in every area of his life. I cancel any attacks of the enemy that will attempt to make him doubt himself or doubt the call that You have on his life. I pray that my husband will always submit to You and fear You above all else in this world. Father, I pray that my future husband knows his identity in You and knows that he is more than a conqueror through Christ Jesus. Give him the strength to face any attacks of the enemy in Jesus' mighty name. I pray that You teach him to walk with boldness and confidence that comes from You alone. I command fear to depart from him now,

In Jesus' name, I pray. Amen.

PRAYER #11

MATURING HIM

1 Corinthians 13:11 ESV; Ephesians 4:13-15 ESV

Ephesians 4:13-15 ESV "until we all attain to the unity of the faith and of the knowledge of the Son of God, to mature manhood, to the measure of the stature of the fullness of Christ, so that we may no longer be children, tossed to and fro by the waves and carried about by every wind of doctrine, by human cunning, by craftiness in deceitful schemes. Rather, speaking the truth in love, we are to grow up in every way into him who is the head, into Christ"

Dear Lord,

I am grateful for the work that You are doing in my life and my future husband's life. I exalt You, King Jesus; and I place You at the center of every area of my life. I pray that You guide and instruct my future husband in Your wisdom and help him to develop an unbreakable bond with You. May his relationship with You grow stronger and stronger every day, and may You continue to shape him into the man of God that You have created him to be.

1 Corinthians 13:11 ESV *"When I was a child, I spoke like a child, I thought like a child, I reasoned like a child. When I became a man, I gave up childish ways."*

Father, I pray for wisdom and self-control for my future husband. Help him to learn to place Your desires for his life above his own desires. I pray You bless him with the spiritual maturity to step into his calling with readiness and power. Help him understand and embrace Your specific plan and purpose for his life.

Lord, I pray that You touch his heart and help him see people the way You see them and love them selflessly and passionately even when it is difficult. Help him to mature in his heart and mind, putting away childish things and stepping into manhood with authority and responsibility. Help him mature in his mindset, communication, and reasoning so that he can lead me and our future family with wisdom and discernment.

Holy Spirit, guide my husband to grow to have the mind of Christ and begin to see things through Your lens. Help him to understand what it means to lead as a man of God. Lord, I pray that when my husband and I get married, we will fully embrace the responsibilities, joys, and tasks of being husband and wife. God, mature his heart to have fun and be playful, but also know when to be serious.

Holy Spirit, fill my husband with Your power, discipline, and boldness, and continue to shape him into a powerhouse for the Kingdom of God. Lord, help him to mature in his character, personality, and outlook on life.

In Jesus' name, I pray. Amen.

SECTION *Two*

DEVELOPMENT IN CHRIST

Philippians 1:6 ESV
"And I am sure of this, that He who began a good work in you will bring it to completion at the day of Jesus Christ."

In this section, you will be focusing on covering your future husband by praying for his development as well as your own. Development in Christ is truly one of the most important things a follower of Christ can receive and learn. There is so much that God can reveal to us once we understand the importance of seeking growth in our relationship with Him. If we never grow to the next level, how can He give us more? If we never conquer the struggles that we face right now in our lives, what makes us think that in our future marriage, we will be able to conquer even more difficult struggles or obstacles?

Let's put it this way, you should be focusing less on growth in marriage and more on growth before marriage. In marriage, you will be responsible not only for yourself but also for your future husband. This is a beautiful union and partnership, but it requires developing a strong relationship with Christ before getting married.

In marriage, each person brings their own development in Christ to the table. What you have learned, what you have experienced, and what the Lord has done in your life are all things that come with you in your newlywed suitcase. But if you don't have any development to bring to the table, then the only things you are bringing into your marriage and giving to your spouse are your past traumas and toxic ways that you never healed from. That is why preparing for your future husband is so important. When the time comes for marriage, you want to be excited and ready to share what the Lord has done for you in your life; you shouldn't be looking at the union of marriage only to share your woes in hopes that your partner can fix you and heal your emotions. Healing will never, and should never come from your spouse but Christ alone. Instead, look at marriage as the opportunity to have a spouse to conquer, triumph, and build a life with.

Development in Christ for your future husband is just as crucial as development in Christ is for you. The man and woman have very different roles within the marriage, and they both bring elements to the table that the other can not offer or fulfill, and that's the beauty of a balanced marriage!

It is crucial to allow yourself to become developed in Christ while praying that your future husband submits to the leading of the Holy Spirit to become a developed man of God. Development in Christ will continue even after you get married; that's the beauty of your walk with God! You never stop walking until you're, ya know, dead.

When you are both wondering when you are ready to take the next step of marriage, listen out for the Word of the Lord. He will tell you and make it abundantly clear; that's why sticking close to Him is so important. How can you hear from someone if you are far away from them? If you want direction, clarity, and guidance from the Lord, but you aren't doing what it takes to draw near to Him and seek Him, you won't hear Him. When you don't hear Him, you don't receive the blessings that come from obeying Him!

James 4:8 ESV *"Draw near to God, and He will draw near to you."*

The process of development is no cakewalk; it can be grueling and, at times, tempting to give up, but guess what? If you give up, you'll never see the results! The harvest you will reap from submitting yourself to the development of the Holy Spirit is unbelievable, He wants to reward you! Funny enough, everything you desire in your life and in your future marriage, is at the other end of you working to allow yourself to be developed in Christ. Oftentimes, this is when people want to give up because they don't want to wait and they aren't willing to put in the work. That is why the divorce rates are outrageously high in today's modern society.

A strange thing begins to happen when you submit yourself to the development of the Holy Spirit; you begin to walk like Him and talk like Him. The Bible makes it very clear that to actually experience growth and advancement in your life, you have to go through the process of renewing your mind. To renew your mind means to replace old ways of thinking with new ways of thinking. Old habits with new ones!

Romans 12:2 ESV *"Do not be conformed to this world, but be transformed by the renewal of your mind, that by testing you may discern what is the will of God, what is good and acceptable and perfect."*

Purpose is revealed in development! If you want to become the woman of God you were created to be and you desire your husband to become the man of God he was created to be, that first starts with development. You don't just suddenly become a man or woman who seeks after God's heart; you both first develop a hunger to chase after all that God has called you to be!

During section two of this prayer book, really press into praying for development in Christ for your future husband as well as for yourself! And guess what? As you are praying for your future husband, you are actually growing close to Christ yourself! Seek Him, and you will find Him! Let's dive in!

PRAYER #12

HIS HEALTH

Jeremiah 33:6 NIV; Isaiah 53:5 NIV; 1 Corinthians 6:19–20

Jeremiah 33:6 NIV "Nevertheless, I will bring health and healing to it; I will heal My people and will let them enjoy abundant peace and security."

Lord,

I thank You for all You have done in my life and my future husband's life. I praise Your name and thank You for being a Healer. I invite You into my life and my future husband's life to heal us in every way possible—mentally, physically, and spiritually. I come before You, Lord, praying for my future husband's health. Father, I come against any sickness in his life, in Jesus' name. Lord, I command any sickness and disease in his body to go right now in the name of Jesus'. I command any sickness in his mind to go right now by the power of the blood of Jesus. I speak health over his life, and I cancel any and all attacks of the enemy right now in Jesus' name. Lord, free him from sickness not only in the mind and the body but also in his relationships. Father, heal my future husband from anything that needs healing in his life. Fill him now with Your supernatural healing power. I pray for healing from his past and detachment from past relationships in Jesus' name.

Isaiah 53:5 NIV *"But He was pierced for our transgressions, He was crushed for our iniquities; the punishment that brought us peace was on Him, and by His wounds we are healed."*

Heal him, Lord, from anything the enemy is using to hold him back from his calling, Father break all strongholds in his life right now, in Jesus' name. God, I pray that he continues to grow a strong and healthy relationship with You as his Lord and Savior. Father, I pray that he has healthy, God-glorifying relationships in his life. I pray that You give my husband an abundance of wisdom in navigating the relationships that he has in his life. God, I pray that my husband and I will have an unbelievably healthy relationship from the time we begin dating to the day we are old and gray in marriage. Lord, I pray my husband is a disciplined advocate for healthy living. I pray that my husband uses wisdom to avoid anything that could harm his body or tempt him to sin. Convict his heart and give him the strength to withstand temptation by Your power, Father. I pray that my husband submits his body to You, Lord, as a sacrifice. I pray that my husband will take his health seriously and be disciplined in how he cares for his mind and body. Finally, I pray that You mend his heart from any wounds,

In Jesus' name. Amen.

PRAYER #13

HUMILITY AND THE FRUITS OF THE SPIRIT

**Colossians 3:12 NIV; Ephesians 4:2 NIV;
Galatians 5:22–23 ESV**

*Colossians 3:12 NIV "Therefore, as God's
chosen people, holy and dearly loved, clothe
yourselves with compassion, kindness, humility,
gentleness and patience."*

*Ephesians 4:2 NIV "Be completely humble and
gentle; be patient, bearing with one another in love."*

Lord,

I pray that my future husband is a man of humility and that everything he does will be rooted in Your love. I pray that You remove any selfishness from his heart and give him an abundance of compassion towards others. Father, I pray that You renew his heart and mind, removing all pride in Jesus' name.

God, I pray that my husband and I will serve each other selflessly within our marriage. Provide us with hearts to serve others with the joy and honor that comes from doing Your work. I pray that in every situation, my husband and I work to respond to each other with patience and humility. Give him Your strength not to grow weary of following You and doing Your work.

Lord, I pray that my husband continues to chase You and apply Your Word to his heart so that the fruits of the Spirit are evident in his life. Give him the discipline to practice love, joy, peace, patience, kindness, goodness, faithfulness, gentleness, and self-control, even when it is challenging. May the fruits of the Spirit be apparent in his life for all to see in Jesus' name.

> **Galatians 5:22-23 ESV** *"But the fruit of the Spirit is love, joy, peace, patience, kindness, goodness, faithfulness, gentleness, self-control; against such things there is no law."*

I pray that my husband will constantly work to make his heart look more like Yours every day. Give him endurance to keep chasing after Your heart, Father. I pray that my husband and I will constantly work to see things from each other's perspective and understanding. I pray that he is never hesitant to express his emotions or thoughts with me as his wife.

Lord, I pray that my future husband is humble and gentle, but I also pray that he is assertive and bold. May he learn the importance of leading with the humility You desire us to operate in. God, may my husband and I learn to prioritize each other as husband and wife and apply the fruits of the Spirit to our marriage.

In Jesus' name, I pray. Amen.

PRAYER #14

HIS FAITH

**Hebrews 11:6 NIV; Proverbs 3:5-6 NIV;
Matthew 21:21-22 NIV**

*Hebrews 11:6 NIV "And without faith it is
impossible to please God, because anyone who
comes to Him must believe that He exists and that
He rewards those who earnestly seek Him."*

Lord,

I come before You, thanking You for the opportunity to increase my faith in You as I wait and pray for my future spouse. I pray that in this season, my future husband and I will not grow weary of waiting on You. Lord, I pray that he and I will press into our faith and have unwavering confidence in Your timing. I speak Jesus over our marriage; I speak Your mighty power into our relationship. Holy Spirit work in and through our marriage in Jesus' name. Father, I pray that my husband will have faith, boldness, and confidence in You like David, a warrior of God with a heart that chases after You. I pray that my husband's faith in You is so strong that he will come against the lies of the enemy when the enemy attempts to attack him. Lord, I pray that my husband knows the power he has access to through Your mighty name. Give him faith to trust what he doesn't understand and the ability to be content with the things he can't change. I pray that my future husband will trust You even in the middle of trials and storms. Father, I pray that You increase his faith in who You are and the relationship he has with You. I pray that, in all his ways, my future husband submits to You and trusts the path that You have set him on.

Matthew 19:26 ESV *"But Jesus looked at them and said, "With man this is impossible, but with God all things are possible."*

Lord, work in his life and grow him into the man You have called him to be. God, I pray that You give him unwavering faith to trust in Your calling on his life. Bless him with undeniable faith that stands defiant against the darkness of this world. Give him endurance, Father, to seek Your presence no matter what he faces in his life and in our marriage. Lord, I declare that my husband and I will be a couple who places their trust in the Lord. I cancel any attacks of the enemy that will attempt to keep our union from coming to fruition. I pray that You will grow my faith and increase my husband's faith so we can stand firm on the battlefield that You have called us to.

In Jesus' mighty name, Amen.

PRAYER #15

RAPID GROWTH

**1 Timothy 4:15 ESV; James 1:2-4 ESV;
Colossians 1:9-10 ESV**

Colossians 1:9-10 ESV "And so, from the day we heard, we have not ceased to pray for you, asking that you may be filled with the knowledge of His will in all spiritual wisdom and understanding, so as to walk in a manner worthy of the Lord, fully pleasing to Him: bearing fruit in every good work and increasing in the knowledge of God"

Dear God,

I thank You for teaching my husband and I to become more like You. Lord, I pray for rapid growth for us both as we both prepare our hearts for marriage. I pray that my husband will have a hunger to grow and learn more about You every day. Lord, show my future husband how to be a man of God who will lead me as his wife and lead our future children. I pray that You place godly men in my husband's life to give him an example of what a man after God looks like. Father, I pray that You give him a teachable spirit that will yield to the conviction and correction of the Holy Spirit. Help my husband and I learn to apply Your correction and instruction to our lives to become more like You. Lord, I ask that You place godly leaders in our lives to mentor and grow us as a couple who is pursuing You.

James 1:2-4 ESV *"Count it all joy, my brothers, when you meet trials of various kinds, for you know that the testing of your faith produces steadfastness. And let steadfastness have its full effect, that you may be perfect and complete, lacking in nothing."*

Father, give my husband and I an abundance of supernatural wisdom and discernment in selecting leaders whom we receive mentorship and spiritual guidance from. Above all else, I pray that my husband and I will submit to Your authority alone and not look to the approval of others. Bless us both with supernatural rapid growth so that we can do the work of the Kingdom effectively and efficiently. Father, I pray for supernatural growth in both our lives for the rest of our lives. I pray for Your increase in Jesus' name. Give my husband and I a heart to change, grow, and apply the Word of God to our lives. Lord, allow us both to take advantage of this season of waiting for each other while we work to become the individuals

You have created us to be within our marriage. I pray that even when we join in marriage, we will continue to grow in all areas of our lives but, most importantly, grow in our relationship with You.

In Jesus' name, I pray. Amen.

PRAYER #16

CLOSENESS TO YOU

**1 Thessalonians 5:17 ESV; Jeremiah 33:3 ESV;
Psalm 73:28 ESV; James 4:8 ESV**

*Psalm 73:28 ESV "But for me it is good to be near
God; I have made the Lord God my refuge, that I
may tell of all Your works."*

Lord,

I thank You, Jesus, for dying on the cross so that we can experience a deep and close relationship with You. Lord, I pray for my future husband and his relationship with You; I pray that he experiences closeness with You all the days of his life. Draw him near to Your heart, Lord, and pull him close to You. Father, I pray that my future husband will chase after You and seek You in all areas of his life. God, I pray that You reveal Yourself to him and bless him with an abundance of revelation that only comes from having a close and intimate relationship with You.

1 Thessalonians 5:17 ESV *"pray without ceasing"*

Jesus, I come before You, asking that You continue to work in my life and my future husband's life and prepare us both for our future. I pray that my future husband is committed to following Your Word and applying it to his life daily. God, I pray that he is a man of obedience and commitment. Within our marriage, I pray that he and I will always place You first and push each other closer to You. I pray that my future husband will work to continue to renew his mind through Your Word.

James 4:8 ESV *"Draw near to God, and He will draw near to you."*

Father, bless my future husband with a heart that is after You and a heart that seeks to please You in everything he does. I pray that we will never sacrifice our time with You in our marriage and will always keep You at the center of our union. Lord, I pray that You mend any wounds that need mending so that our hearts are fully ready for the blessing of marriage. I pray that my husband will never stop pursuing You when he is searching for answers, direction, or peace. Lord, teach him to become a prayer warrior who will fight for our future family in Jesus' name. I pray that my husband and I will experience what it means to be intimate with You within our marriage.

In Jesus' name, Amen.

PRAYER #17

SELF-CONTROL

Proverbs 25:28 NLT; James 4:7 NIV; 2 Timothy 1:7 ESV

Proverbs 25:28 NLT "A person without self-control is like a city with broken-down walls."

Dear Lord,

I thank You for giving us so many examples of Your discipline and self- control within the Word of God. I know that to walk in purpose, confidence, power, and authority means to exercise self–control and discipline daily. I pray for an abundance of self–control for my future husband and I as we learn to live a life after You.

I pray right now, Father, that You empower my future husband and show him the importance of exercising self–control in every area of his life, so that he may live a life that is pleasing to You. I pray that You show him how to have self–control in his thoughts, his relationships, and his communication. Father, I pray that he will pick up his cross and deny his flesh daily so that he may become the influential leader within the Kingdom of God that You have called Him to be. I pray that he will lead other men and show them what it means to be a man living a life of self–control through the Word of God. I pray that he will protect what he looks at and thinks about to exercise purity in his body and mind.

2 Timothy 1:7 ESV *"For God gave us a spirit not of fear but of power and love and self-control."*

Lord, continue to mold him and raise him up to be invincible against the attacks of the enemy so that he and I may run this race of life together, fully committed and rooted in the Word of God. Father, give my future husband a desire to continue chasing after You all the days of his life. I pray that he will not grow weary of discipline but embrace it to become fully complete in You. I pray that my future husband is encouraged by the fruits of his discipline and continues to work to grow in his self–control. If there is any area of his life where he lacks self–control, Lord, I pray that You will convict his heart and show him the proper tools to live a disciplined life. Lord, thank You for Your correction, and guidance.

In Jesus' name, I pray. Amen.

PRAYER #18

UNDERSTANDING LOVE

1 Corinthians 13:4-13 NIV

1 Corinthians 13:4-13 NIV "Love is patient, love is kind. It does not envy, it does not boast, it is not proud. It does not dishonor others, it is not self-seeking, it is not easily angered, it keeps no record of wrongs. Love does not delight in evil but rejoices with the truth. It always protects, always trusts, always hopes, always perseveres."

Dear Lord,

I come before You, thanking You and praising You for Your love that You show us every single day. Lord, I pray that my future husband and I learn the true meaning of love and practice loving others the way that You love us.

> **1 Corinthians 13:13** *"And now these three remain: faith, hope and love. But the greatest of these is love."*

To love in marriage means to sacrifice and to serve each other with patience and joy. I pray that You prepare both of our hearts to serve and love each other in a way that glorifies You, Father. I pray that in our marriage, my future husband and I will learn how to sacrifice for each other in every way—physically, spiritually, and emotionally. Prepare my future husband to lead me as his wife and to lead our future family in the discipline of love. I speak unity over our future marriage, and I pray that we will both uplift each other and speak the truth in love, compassion, and understanding. Give us both eyes to see each other the way that You see us Father. I pray that You touch my future husband's heart and fill him with Your love so that he will know how to show Your love to those around him. God, show him what it means to be rooted in love and mature his heart to learn how to show his love and emotions to me intimately as his wife. Lord, I pray that our love as husband and wife will grow each and every day as we grow closer to You. Lord, I pray that my husband knows how to show love and how to receive it, and I pray that You heal him from any hurt that may have come from a lack of love.

In Jesus' name, Amen.

PRAYER #19

INTIMACY WITH CHRIST

John 15:4-6 ESV; Jeremiah 33:3 ESV; Psalm 63:1-11 ESV

John 15:4-6 ESV "I am the vine; you are the branches. Whoever abides in Me and I in him, he it is that bears much fruit, for apart from Me you can do nothing. If anyone does not abide in Me he is thrown away like a branch and withers; and the branches are gathered, thrown into the fire, and burned."

Dear Lord,

I thank You for Your sacrifice to bring us close to Your heart. I pray that my future husband will have an unbreakable bond with You and I pray that he will seek Your guidance throughout his life. Please help him Father, to submit himself to You and Your instruction. Lord, teach him to be humble and to seek intimacy with You so that his relationship with You grows stronger every day, even in marriage.

Jeremiah 33:3 ESV *"Call to Me and I will answer You, and will tell you great and hidden things that you have not known."*

Psalm 63:3-4 ESV *"Because your steadfast love is better than life, my lips will praise You. So I will bless You as long as I live; in Your name I will lift up my hands."*

I pray that his relationship with You will be evident in his life and that he will worship You with discipline and choose to glorify You through sacrifice. When he faces trials, I pray he will turn to You and find strength in Your Word and in Your presence. I pray he will strive to live a life that pleases You and reflects Your image. Direct his steps and guide him as he submits his life to You. May he pursue intimacy with You as an individual and as my future husband. Help us to seek You together as husband and wife.

In Jesus' name, Amen.

PRAYER #20

LIVING A SURRENDERED LIFE TO CHRIST

Matthew 16:24-25 ESV; Ephesians 6:10-18 ESV

Matthew 16:24-25 ESV "Then Jesus told his disciples, 'If anyone would come after Me, let him deny himself and take up his cross and follow Me.' For whoever would save his life will lose it, but whoever loses his life for My sake will find it."

Jesus,

Thank You for sending the Holy Spirit to lead and guide us. I pray that my future husband will understand what it means to be surrendered to the Holy Spirit. I pray that he will learn to pick up his cross and follow You, even when faced with significant obstacles. I pray that he will sacrifice his mind, spirit, and body to You daily so that You may move in and through his life. I pray that he will submit to Your will and the leading of the Holy Spirit, even when he doesn't understand or when he feels uncertain of what You are calling him to do.

Father, I come against any confusion in his life and any lies the enemy may use to distract him from hearing Your voice, Holy Spirit. Father, give him clarity to discern Your voice from his thoughts; I pray that he will distinctly know Your voice and obey Your words. I pray that he will crucify his flesh daily and understand the importance of getting into the Word and seeking Your voice first thing in the morning. Holy Spirit, give him the strength to submit his flesh to what You are calling him to do.

Ephesians 6:10 ESV *"Finally, be strong in the Lord and in the strength of His might. Put on the whole armor of God, that you may be able to stand against the schemes of the devil."*

Father, I pray that he pursues the life that You have called him to live, and I pray for boldness to walk out that life despite any fears and obstacles that may try to slow him down. Holy Spirit, continue to reveal his purpose to him in Your timing, and I pray that he trusts You while he waits for You to reveal Your plan to him.

Thank You, Lord, for his diligence in pursuing You, and I pray that he will learn to know You and love You more every day.

In Jesus' name, Amen.

PRAYER #21

PURITY

**Psalm 119:9 NIV; Colossians 3:5 NIV;
1 Corinthians 6:18 ESV; Titus 2:11-14 ESV**

Titus 2:11-14 ESV "For the grace of God has appeared, bringing salvation for all people, training us to renounce ungodliness and worldly passions, and to live self-controlled, upright, and godly lives in the present age, waiting for our blessed hope, the appearing of the glory of our great God and Savior Jesus Christ, who gave Himself for us to redeem us from all lawlessness and to purify for Himself a people for His own possession who are zealous for good works."

Lord,

I thank You for the gift of purity and for the forgiveness that was made possible through the sacrifice of Your Son on the cross. I pray that my future husband will have a deep desire to pursue purity and that he will be committed to living a life that is pleasing to You. May he have a hunger for Your Word and obedience to follow Your instructions in all things. I pray that he will value purity and work diligently to guard his heart and mind against anything that might compromise it. Help him to be strong and courageous in the face of temptation, and give him the wisdom to make wise choices that will honor You and bless our marriage.

Colossians 3:5 NIV *"Put to death, therefore, whatever belongs to your earthly nature: sexual immorality, impurity, lust, evil desires and greed, which is idolatry."*

Father, I pray that he will also practice purity in his communication and meditation. I pray that if there is any sexual immorality in his life, he will renounce it, uproot it, repent, and turn from his ways to pursue You. Lord, I pray that he diligently pursues the purity that You desire for him and unlocks new power in You because of his submission and devotion to You, Your Word, and the way of purity.

Psalm 119:9 NIV *"How can a young person stay on the path of purity? By living according to Your Word."*

I pray that my future husband's public life aligns with his private life. Please convict his heart of any impurities and unclean ways that are not pleasing to You. Father, I pray that my future husband will pursue purity in his mind by meditating on You and Your call on his life. Even after we get married, I pray that we will never stop seeking purity within our union. God, I pray that my future husband will use the blessings You have given him to bless those around him. Please lead and guide him on his path.

In Jesus' name, I pray, Amen.

SECTION

Three

LEADERSHIP IN MARRIAGE

Luke 12:48 ESV
"Everyone to whom much was given, of him much will be required, and from him to whom they entrusted much, they will demand the more."

Focusing On Becoming The Leader
That You Would Want To Marry

In the third and final section of this prayer book, you will be taking the time to dive into praying for your future husband's leadership not only within your future marriage, but also within his current community. Whether we realize it or not, leadership is the key to success in any capacity. I know it might sound a little weird to use the word "success" when it comes to marriage, but isn't that what we all desire? A successful marriage?

The answer is yes! The truth is that the Lord desires for us to have a successful marriage in every way. A successful marriage pushes others around them toward Christ and serves as an example of the bond between Christ and the body of Christ. A successful marriage involves a man and a woman who both boldly approach the throne of God, interceding on each other's behalf. A successful marriage is a man and woman leading each other back to the Word of God and reminding each other of His promises when life gets tough. A successful marriage uplifts and encourages one another in love. A marriage that is of the Lord is a safe and intimate place where a man and a woman can grow together in faithfulness and the way of love.

Now, all of these things sound amazing and beautiful, but to obtain these lovely things, there has to be a foundation of leadership. You can not experience the beauty of marriage without building on the foundation of leadership first. It all begins by answering the call of the Lord and realizing that your way just won't cut it. Leadership then continues by submitting to the ultimate leader, the Holy Spirit. Listening and obeying the Word of God, even when it's tough, is the real and honest truth of leadership that is necessary in a world of broken marriages. Discipline and leadership will take you back to the Word of God to root yourself in His promises and peace when you feel warfare rising against your marriage.

Marriage is hardly ever just only about two people. When two are joined together as husband and wife, the purpose and goal is to do more, reach more, and accomplish more for the Kingdom of God. Your future marriage is an offering to the Lord of two people standing up together, saying they are ready to be used by the King for His glory and purpose. When a couple comes together in marriage and publicly declares their commitment to each other with Christ at the center, they invite the blessings of the Lord into their marriage. A marriage built on the foundation of Jesus Christ serves as a powerful example to others, encouraging and uplifting them to follow the Word of God above all else.

And when I speak of leadership, I am not just speaking of leadership for your future husband, but also for yourself as a woman of God even before marriage. A woman of leadership is abundantly powerful and is honestly a rare find in today's modern society. To be a woman who has her own independent relationship with her Father and knows how to fight on behalf of herself, her husband, and her family with authority is frightening to the enemy and the kingdom of darkness.

Somehow, in our culture, we have found rest in putting the blame on our men in society. We've gotten comfortable with pointing the finger and not holding ourselves accountable as women. The questions that we should be asking ourselves as women are: how am I leading? Do I know the Word of God for myself? Do I have an independent relationship with the Lord? Am I speaking life into those around me? Am I submitting myself to the leadership of the Holy Spirit? Am I obeying the

Word of God? Am I studying the Word of God every day? How is my prayer life? Have I given up the things of the world? Am I seeking the Lord and inviting Him in every area of my life? Am I seeking attention from men, or am I confident in my identity in Christ? Am I serving others around me? Am I serving and leading in ministry? Am I content in my singleness?

The list goes on, but those are just a few questions to ask yourself to do a self-evaluation to find out where you are and if you are ready for marriage. This list isn't to overwhelm you but to encourage you to use this time wisely and to let you know that this season you're in serves a purpose! This is a beautiful season to really discover your relationship with Christ for yourself. This is a time to build your life on a firm foundation and not wait for your future husband to do it for you.

We as women should never wait for our husbands to follow Christ before we do; we should already be following Christ before marriage to discern the type of man of God we should marry.

Here is a truth to chew on: God will give you a husband who can lead you. So, if you begin elevating your own leadership before you even get married, God will provide you with an even stronger man to lead you. So, the bottom line is if you want to marry a leader, you first have to be a leader.

Leadership should be the goal for your future marriage because leadership will not only help lead others, but it will lead your marriage and your future family. When trials come, and they will come, leadership and discipline is what will get you both on your knees and into the Word of God. Leadership is what will make you stronger when trials come and not crumble when life gets difficult.

PRAYER #22

WISDOM & DISCERNMENT

James 1:5-8 NIV; Proverbs 1:7 ESV; Philippians 1:9-10 NIV

*Philippians 1:9 NIV "And this is my prayer:
that your love may abound more and more in
knowledge and depth of insight, so that you may
be able to discern what is best and may be pure
and blameless for the day of Christ"*

Lord,

Thank you for the blessing of Your wisdom. Your Word says we have not because we ask not, so I ask that You pour out Your supernatural wisdom on my future husband and I. Father, I pray that my future husband will apply Your Word to his life, and display the wisdom You have given him through his actions. May Your wisdom guide and influence our decisions in our relationship and marriage. I pray that he never stops seeking You for understanding and wisdom, my prayer is that he relies on You for strength and guidance.

Proverbs 1:7 ESV *"The fear of the Lord is the beginning of knowledge; fools despise wisdom and instruction."*

Lord, anoint his words and give him discernment to know when to speak and what to say. May he be rooted in Your humility so that the Holy Spirit can move through him wherever he goes. I pray he uses his voice to speak the truth with power and authority in Your name, Jesus.

James 1:5 NIV *"If any of you lacks wisdom, you should ask God, who gives generously to all without finding fault, and it will be given to you"*

I pray that even when unsure, he seeks Your guidance and understanding. God, give him a hunger and fire to pursue Your wisdom and learn as much as he can from Your Word. When the enemy attempts to confuse him, I pray he turns away from all distractions to hear Your voice clearly. Holy Spirit, guide his decisions so that he is operating fully in Your will and not operating outside the plan You have prepared for him. I pray that You provide him with supernatural discernment Father; show him Lord how to submit his ways to You.

In Jesus' name, I pray. Amen.

PRAYER #23

TRUSTING YOU

Proverbs 3:5–6 ESV; Isaiah 26:3–4 ESV; Jeremiah 29:11 NLT

*Proverbs 3:5-6 ESV "Trust in the Lord with
all your heart, and do not lean on your own
understanding. In all your ways acknowledge Him,
and He will make straight your paths."*

Lord,

I know that learning to trust You can be difficult, especially in the midst of adversity, but I pray that my future husband's faith is bold, solid, and unwavering. I pray that You give him bulletproof faith so that later in life, he and I can draw our strength from the well of our faith within our marriage. Lord, I pray that my husband learns what it means to trust You and walk in the faith that You command us to walk in. Grow and mature his heart, Lord, to learn how to continue to follow You even when he doesn't understand the situation he is facing.

> **Isaiah 26:3-4 ESV** *"You keep him in perfect peace whose mind is stayed on You, because he trusts in You. Trust in the Lord forever, for the Lord God is an Everlasting Rock."*

I come against any fear in his life in Jesus' name; I pray that he will run to You in moments of doubt, fear, and confusion. Give my husband fearless faith to lean into the promises of Your Word. I pray that my husband will take refuge in You alone for everything in his life. Father, give him the faith to be obedient to what You are calling him to do so that he may please You in every area of his life. I pray that our future household will be built on the foundation of bold faith that trusts in You.

> **Jeremiah 29:11 NIV** *"For I know the plans I have for you," declares the Lord, "plans to prosper you and not to harm you, plans to give you hope and a future."*

I pray that when the enemy attempts to attack his faith, he will turn to the Word of God and remember what You have already spoken over his life. I pray that You give my husband an abundance of supernatural faith so that he can lead our future family straight to Your will and plan. Strengthen and sharpen my future husband's spiritual gifts, Lord, I pray that You provide him with situations to practice and use the gifts that You have given him. I command all fear to go from him now in Jesus name. Holy Spirit, fill his heart with confidence in the plan that You have for him. Fill him up, and equip him to do Your work, not only in our ministry but within our future family.

In Jesus' name, Amen.

PRAYER #24

GODLY RELATIONSHIPS

Proverbs 27:17 ESV; Job 42:10 ESV; Proverbs 11:14 ESV

Proverbs 27:17 ESV "Iron sharpens iron, and one man sharpens another"

Lord,

I thank You for the gift of relationships in our lives. I pray that my future husband has a strong and godly male figure in his life who can serve as an example of what it means to be a surrendered man after Christ. I pray that my future husband has a strong and positive bond with his father and that their relationship is built on You.

Proverbs 11:14 ESV *"Where there is no guidance, a people falls, but in an abundance of counselors there is safety."*

Lord, I pray that if my future husband does not have a relationship with his father, You will bring godly men into his life to fill that important role. I pray that my husband will not find his sole identity in his earthly father but in You alone as his Creator and Savior. Lord, I pray that my husband will experience godly friendships overflowing with brotherhood and loyalty. Lord, I pray that You fulfill his desire for friendship by placing other men in his life who will encourage and uplift him.

Job 42:10 ESV *"And the Lord restored the fortunes of Job, when he had prayed for his friends. And the Lord gave Job twice as much as he had before."*

Father, I pray that his friendships are genuine, like iron sharpening iron, keeping each other accountable and strong. I pray that his friendships will last a lifetime, even when we get married and have children in the future. I speak Jesus over our friend group in marriage, and I pray that our circle will grow as we grow closer to You. Lord, I pray that our future friend group will be filled with laughter, love, and support as we point each other toward the cross. God, I pray that he practices being a supportive friend in the relationships You have blessed him with, and

Lord, show him how to serve his friends well. Lord, I pray for Your blessings in his life and the lives of his friends. I pray that You surround my future husband with godly men who will pour out their hearts in prayer for him and our marriage one day.

Thank You for the gift of friendship and community.

In Jesus' name, I pray. Amen.

PRAYER #25

CONSISTENCY, DILIGENCE, & ENDURANCE

2 Timothy 3:16–17 ESV; Hebrews 12:1–4 ESV; Romans 5:3–4 ESV

2 Timothy 3:16-17 ESV "All Scripture is breathed out by God and profitable for teaching, for reproof, for correction, and for training in righteousness, that the man of God may be complete, equipped for every good work."

Lord,

I thank You for my future husband. I thank You for his life and the blessing he already is to me. I pray for him in this season as we prepare our hearts for each other, that You will mold our hearts and renew our minds so that we will be ready for the gift of marriage.

Father, teach my future husband to run with endurance so that even in the midst of a storm, his faith will not waver or crumble, but grow stronger. Lord, I pray that You teach my future husband to be consistent and diligent in all he does, honoring You with his faithfulness. Lord, mold him to be a man of his word who follows through on his promises. I pray that he learns to be a hard worker who chases after what You are calling him to do, even if it is challenging or difficult. I pray that he grows into a diligent worker who pushes forward, even if he doesn't see the desired results. I pray he has a teachable spirit to hear and obey Your instructions.

Romans 5:3-4 ESV *"Not only that, but we rejoice in our sufferings, knowing that suffering produces endurance, and endurance produces character, and character produces hope"*

Lord, I also pray for patience in our marriage and that my future husband has a patient heart with me as his wife. I pray that our marriage will be built on consistency, diligence, and endurance as we work daily to ensure that our love continues to grow even through trials. I pray that he will never stop pursuing me in marriage and that our romance and connection will grow stronger every day. Lord, I pray for consistency in his work life and that he honors You in how hard he works for You, himself, and our family.

Hebrews 12:1-4 ESV *"Let us also lay aside every weight, and sin which clings so closely, and let us run with endurance the race that is set before us, looking to Jesus, the Founder and Perfecter of our faith."*

Lord, I pray that my husband will exercise wisdom in balancing work, family, and time with You. May he exercise wisdom in his actions and emotions and have a sound mind as the leader of our household. Make his mind and path straight, Father, and give him Your clarity. I pray that he will run with endurance and be encouraged and motivated to do the work You have set out for him to complete. I also pray that my future husband is consistent and diligent in his prayer life and that no matter what he is facing he never ceases to pray. I pray that my husband is intentional about listening to Your voice.

In Jesus' name, I pray, Amen.

PRAYER #26

LEADERSHIP

**John 13:13-17 ESV; Matthew 20:26-28 ESV;
Philippians 2:3-4 ESV**

*John 13:14-15 ESV "If I then, your Lord and
Teacher, have washed your feet, you also ought
to wash one another's feet. For I have given you
an example, that you also should do just as I have
done to you."*

Lord,

I thank You for showing us through Your Word what true leadership looks like because of the example of Your life here on earth. I pray that You continue to show my future husband and I what true leadership looks like. Lord, I pray that my husband will continue chasing You for guidance and leadership in his life. Please continue to prepare his heart to lead his ministry and our future family. I pray he will learn to lead with humility, love, compassion, patience, kindness, power, authority, and integrity. Teach him Your ways and principles, Father. I pray that he will continue to learn more about You to become more like You every day. I also pray that my future husband will learn how to serve those around him and learn to serve me as his wife as I learn to serve him.

Matthew 20:28 ESV *"Even as the Son of Man came not to be served but to serve, and to give his life as a ransom for many."*

Philippians 2:3-4 ESV *"Do nothing from selfish ambition or conceit, but in humility count others more significant than yourselves. Let each of you look not only to his own interests, but also to the interests of others."*

I pray that my future husband will lean on the guidance of the Holy Spirit for direction and wisdom. God, I pray that You raise him up to be the mighty man of God that You have created him to be. Father, I pray that he will desire to lead well by remaining close to You for correction, conviction, and direction. I pray that he and I will work as a unit, both chasing after You. I pray that You give him an abundance of discernment and boldness as the leader and protector of our household. Lord, I pray that You mold us into the leaders this generation needs and guide us both as we step into leadership.

In Jesus' name, I pray, Amen.

PRAYER #27

FLEEING FROM THE ENEMY & RESISTING TEMPTATION

James 4:7 NIV; 1 Corinthians 10:13 ESV; Ephesians 6:16 ESV

1 Corinthians 10:13 ESV "No temptation has overtaken you that is not common to man. God is faithful, and He will not let you be tempted beyond your ability, but with the temptation He will also provide the way of escape, that you may be able to endure it"

Lord,

I come before You, thanking You for the tools You have given us to fight the warfare in this world. I know that no temptation is too great because You have power and authority over all, Jesus!

James 4:7 NIV *"Submit yourselves, then, to God. Resist the devil, and he will flee from you."*

Thank You for always giving us a way out of temptation and giving us the example of living a life of discipline. Lord, I pray for an outpouring of discipline for my future husband to bulletproof his mind and learn the tools You have given him to resist the enemy and stand firm in all he does. Lord, I pray that my future husband will practice resisting the enemy every day of his life. Give him Your strength and discipline to submit his flesh to Your commandments. No temptation is too great or strong because You have conquered every temptation and given us the authority to do the same in Jesus' name.

Ephesians 6:16 ESV *"In all circumstances take up the shield of faith, with which you can extinguish all the flaming darts of the evil one"*

I know that You always provide a way out of every temptation, but I pray You give my husband the willpower and steadfastness to choose the way out and not give the enemy dominion over his life. I pray that he lives a life of freedom in You, Father. I come against and rebuke any sexual immorality and perversion in his life in Jesus' name. I pray that he will make the decision to be a man of God who will honor You in what he looks at, thinks about, and acts on. Lord, I pray that You show him how to break any and all soul ties that he may have from past relationships or sexual encounters, if he has any. Lord, I pray that he will respect and honor me as his future wife, even right now, by saving himself sexually for marriage. Jesus, I pray that he has the mindset and discipline to guard his eyes and mind as if he were already married.

I pray that he will be so dedicated to You and Your Word that he fights to resist all attacks from the enemy. I pray he doesn't even give attention to temptation or play with fire. I pray that whenever he is tempted, he will exercise discipline by bringing his thoughts into captivity and removing himself from the situation that is tempting him. Give him the eyes and discernment to identify any distractions and attacks attempting to make him stumble and fall. I declare that my husband is free from all sexual immorality in Jesus' name. I declare that my husband will live a pure life in Jesus' name. I declare that my husband will resist the devil daily in Jesus' name. Show my future husband how to surrender daily and die to the desires of his flesh.

In Jesus' name, I pray and declare, Amen.

PRAYER #28

LETTING GO OF THE PAST

**Proverbs 4:25–27 ESV; Isaiah 43:18–19 ESV;
Philippians 3:13–14 NLT**

*Philippians 3:13-14 NLT "No, dear brothers and
sisters, I have not achieved it, but I focus on this
one thing: Forgetting the past and looking forward
to what lies ahead, I press on to reach the end of
the race and receive the heavenly prize for which
God, through Christ Jesus, is calling us."*

Lord,

I pray for my future husband right now. I thank You for the freedom that You offer us, Jesus. I pray that my future husband will experience freedom in You from anything in his past. If there is anything in his past that is holding him back from the future that You have planned for him, I pray that he will renounce it and break off any ties to it in Jesus' name. Lord, I thank You for the opportunity to start fresh because of what You did on the cross. Father, Your Word says, "Where the Spirit of the Lord is, there is freedom," so I pray that Your Spirit will flood his life and consume all darkness in Jesus' name. I pray that You will heal him from his past and break off any emotional ties that he may have. Lord, I pray that my husband walks in the freedom that comes from You alone.

Isaiah 43:18-19 ESV *"Remember not the former things, nor consider the things of old. Behold, I am doing a new thing"*

Proverbs 4:25 ESV *"Let your eyes look directly forward, and your gaze be straight before you."*

If anything in his past is clouding his judgment, I pray that he receives wisdom and clarity from You. I pray that he will never put his past over our marriage, and I pray that he will let go of the past and press towards the future that You have for him. Father, before we unite in marriage, I pray that You heal him from anything the enemy will try to use to divide us in our union. I pray that my husband will set his mind on things above instead of meditating on earthly things or things of the past. Give my future husband the endurance to press forward and run the race that You have set out for him. I pray that You show my future husband how to uproot things, people, and emotions from his past, so that he may be fully healthy and ready when it is time for us to join together in marriage.

In Jesus' name. Amen.

PRAYER #29

OUR FINANCES

Job 22:21 NIV; 3 John 1:2 ESV; Colossians 3:23-24 ESV

Colossians 3:23-24 ESV "Whatever you do, work heartily, as for the Lord and not for men, knowing that from the Lord you will receive the inheritance as your reward. You are serving the Lord Christ."

Dear Lord,

I thank You for the abundance of blessings You have showered upon my future husband and I. I am grateful for everything we have, and I pray that You will continue to bless us in all aspects of our lives. I ask that You touch our finances and help us to be generous givers to Your Kingdom and Your children. May we have a heart willing to give without hesitation so that we may be Your light wherever we go.

Lord, I pray that my husband and I will bless others with our giving, not only in our finances but also in how we give our love and time. I pray for Your blessings over our finances in Jesus' name so that we may bless others through the blessings You have poured onto us. I pray for an abundance of blessings over our lives and marriage as we chase You and Your Kingdom, Father. I pray that we will have intangible riches within our marriage and future family, and that Your love and joy will overflow within our hearts and household.

Job 22:21 NIV *"Submit to God and be at peace with Him; in this way prosperity will come to you."*

Father, I pray that my husband and I will rely on You for our needs and desires. I pray for supernatural wisdom and clarity as we navigate and manage our finances. Lord, I pray that You show us how to multiply our finances so that we can be an even bigger force and blessing in the Kingdom of God. I come against and rebuke the spirit of mammon and poverty in our lives in Jesus' name. Father, give us Your generous heart and help us always give and serve with a cheerful heart. Help us to honor You in every area of our lives, including our finances.

In Jesus' name, I pray for an exceptionally generous heart for my future husband and I to meet the needs of others wherever we go. May we be a blessing to those around us and bring glory to Your name.

Amen

PRAYER #30

PREPARING HIS HEART FOR MARRIAGE

Genesis 2:24 ESV; Ephesians 5:25 ESV; Matthew 19:6 NIV

Ephesians 5:25 ESV "Husbands, love your wives, as Christ loved the church and gave Himself up for her."

Lord,

I come before You, thanking You and praising You for my future husband. I thank You for the man he already is and for the man You are molding him to become. I pray that You will continue to prepare his heart not only for marriage but also to lead our future family with humility and strength. I pray that You transform his heart to look more like Yours every day. Touch his heart, Father, and show him what it means to be a surrendered man who chases and follows You. I pray that You heal my husband from anything in his past that would keep him from being ready for marriage. Lord, I pray that my husband cannot wait to marry me and that he does not feel pressure but only excitement and confidence in You.

> **Genesis 2:24 ESV** *"Therefore a man shall leave his father and his mother and hold fast to his wife, and they shall become one flesh."*

I pray that our marriage will be genuine and filled with love and excitement throughout our years together. I pray that he and I will fall more and more in love with each other each day as we grow closer to You. I pray that my future husband and I will understand what love is and what it isn't by the example You have given us through Your Word. Help us both to fully submit to Your Word so that we may learn to love each other the way You created us to love each other. Lord, guide my future husband in becoming a man who is sensitive to the Holy Spirit's leading and show him how to love with patience, understanding, and gentleness. I pray that within our marriage, we will experience oneness, intimacy, and unity drenched in love and faithfulness to each other.

Matthew 19:6 NIV *"So they are no longer two, but one flesh. Therefore what God has joined together, let no one separate."*

I pray that You prepare his heart for my quirks, needs, and desires. And I pray, Father, that You will prepare my heart to love my husband the way he needs and desires to be loved. Lord, continue to prepare us and show us how to prepare our minds and hearts for the marriage You have for us. Above all else, I pray that our marriage is Holy Spirit–led so that we may honor You in the way we trust and follow You. I pray that he and I will submit to Your leading and timing within our relationship.

In Jesus' name, I pray, Amen.

PRAYER #31

OUR WEDDING

Philippians 4:6 NIV; Psalm 145:7 NIV; Psalm 126:3 NIV

Psalm 145:7 NIV "They celebrate Your abundant goodness and joyfully sing of Your righteousness."

Lord,

Thank You for preparing my heart and my future husband's heart to unite and glorify You in marriage one day. I pray my future husband and I will always boldly pursue You. Father, I uplift our wedding day and I cancel any attacks of the enemy against us and our wedding right now, in Jesus' name. Lord, I pray that You will be glorified throughout our wedding ceremony, from start to finish. Father, I pray that the presence of God will be in and throughout every moment of our wedding and reception. Lord, I pray that our guests will encounter You and Your presence throughout our wedding festivities, in Jesus' name.

I pray for unity between my husband's family and my family, and I pray that both sides will join together in harmony, joy, peace, and excitement. I pray that we will have their love and support throughout the entire process of planning our wedding. I speak Your peace, Father, over our wedding day and even the planning leading up to the wedding. I pray for an outpouring of Your blessings on our special day and that our wedding will be everything my future husband and I have ever dreamed of and more. I come against any stress that tries to steal the joy of our wedding, and I pray that it will be a beautiful representation of Your love, Father.

Philippians 4:6 NIV *"Do not be anxious about anything, but in every situation, by prayer and petition, with thanksgiving, present your requests to God."*

I pray that every moment of our wedding will run smoothly without any complications or issues. Father, anoint my future husband and I as we publicly declare to serve and love each other as husband and wife. God, I pray that our wedding will be a celebration of Your goodness and faithfulness. We thank You, Father, for the opportunity to celebrate our union as husband and wife. I pray that You will be at the center of our wedding and that our union will lead others to You.

In Jesus' name, I pray, Amen.

PRAYER #32

OUR MARRIAGE

Ecclesiastes 4:9–12 NLT; Romans 12:9–12 NLT

Ecclesiastes 4:9-12 NLT "Two people are better off than one, for they can help each other succeed. If one person falls, the other can reach out and help. But someone who falls alone is in real trouble. Likewise, two people lying close together can keep each other warm. But how can one be warm alone? A person standing alone can be attacked and defeated, but two can stand back-to-back and conquer. Three are even better, for a triple-braided cord is not easily broken."

Dear Lord,

I thank You for the gift of marriage and the unity and support that marriage provides. I pray that our marriage will represent You in every way, Father. God, I pray our marriage will serve as an example to others of a man and woman who both submitted themselves to the Lord and trusted His timing. Father, I pray for an outpouring of Your blessings on our marriage so that we may be a blessing to others. I pray that my future husband and I will learn to love and support each other by submitting ourselves to Your Word and instructions. I speak patience and gentleness over our marriage, and I pray that everything we do for each other will be rooted in love.

Romans 12:10-12 NLT *"Love each other with genuine affection, and take delight in honoring each other. Never be lazy, but work hard and serve the Lord enthusiastically. Rejoice in our confident hope. Be patient in trouble, and keep on praying."*

Father, I pray that our communication will be effective and understanding, full of patience and sensitivity. I also pray that our marriage will be filled with joy, laughter, excitement, and service to each other. Even through times of opposition, I pray that my future husband and I will laugh and enjoy life together, no matter the obstacles we face, because of our steadfast faith in You. Father, in my husband's low moments, I pray that I will learn to uplift and support him. I pray that my husband will learn to uplift and encourage me in my low moments and through tough times. I pray for oneness within our marriage and that my husband and I will be on the same page with our thinking and decision-making in every way imaginable.

I pray that my husband will know me and never stop pursuing me to get to know me more and more as the years go by. I pray that You inspire us with new creative ways to show how much we love each other. Holy Spirit, continue to guide my future husband and I as we work to become the man and woman You created us to be. Father, I pray that my husband and I will learn from each other and push each other to grow closer to You. I pray for an abundance of passion and energy within our relationship and that our intimacy will always be fresh, new, and exciting. Draw us close to each other in intimacy, Lord. I speak Jesus over every inch of our marriage, Father.

In Jesus' name, I pray. Amen.

PRAYER #33

LOVING EACH OTHER

**Ephesians 5:25-28 NIV; Ephesians 5:33 NLT;
Colossians 3:19 ESV; Ecclesiastes 4:9-11 NLT**

*Ephesians 5:25-28 NIV "Husbands, love your
wives, just as Christ loved the church and gave
Himself up for her to make her holy, cleansing
her by the washing with water through the Word,
and to present her to Himself as a radiant church,
without stain or wrinkle or any other blemish, but
holy and blameless. In this same way, husbands
ought to love their wives as their own bodies. He
who loves his wife loves himself."*

Lord,

I thank You for the example of love You have given us through Your sacrifice on the cross. I thank You, Father, for loving me and never leaving or forsaking me. Lord, I pray that You continue to show me the true meaning of unconditional love so that I may represent You in how I love others and my future husband. Lord, I pray that You will show my husband and I how to love each other the way You designed us to love in marriage through sacrifice, service, and love. I pray that my future husband and I will serve each other willingly and joyfully, without hesitation.

Ephesians 5:33 NLT *"So again I say, each man must love his wife as he loves himself, and the wife must respect her husband."*

For my husband, I pray that You soften his heart and show him how to lead and love me in the same way You lead and love the body of Christ. God, I pray that my husband will love me as he loves himself and honor and respect me as his wife. Strengthen him as the leader and protector of our future marriage and family. I pray that You show him and teach him how to be a man after God and a warrior who is fully submitted to the leadership of Christ. I pray my husband will lead me with a gentle, humble, and tender heart. Lord, I pray that our love for each other is evident through our communication and actions and that our marriage is everything You designed a godly marriage to be and more. Lord, I pray that my husband and I will be effortlessly faithful to each other because of the foundation we built on You and Your Word. I speak faithfulness and loyalty over our marriage, leaving no room for the enemy's schemes. I pray that my future husband is sensitive to my heart, feelings, and emotions as his wife.

Colossians 3:19 ESV *"Husbands, love your wives, and do not be harsh with them."*

Father, I pray that our greatest ministry as husband and wife will be our marriage and our future family. I pray that we will prioritize each other over outside tasks and be intentional about soaking up the little moments to help us bond and feel connected. God, I pray that the joy of the Lord will be our strength as we minister to each other and to others. Father, I pray that my future husband and I will be eager to work alongside each other as we do the work of our Father.

In Jesus' name, I pray, Amen.

BONUS PRAYER

BECOMING HER

Proverbs 31:10~31 ESV; Proverbs 31:11~12

Proverbs 31:30 ESV "Charm is deceitful, and beauty is vain, but a woman who fears the Lord is to be praised."

Thank You Lord,

For blessing me with the desire to become a wife. I submit myself to You fully to become the woman You have created me to be. Lord, I pray that You continue to mold my heart to look more like Yours so that I may love my husband the way You love him and cherish him. Father, I pray that I will practice humility by submitting to my husband and supporting him as the leader of our household. I pray that my husband constantly works to become the leader of our household that You created him to be, so that he may lead our marriage and family in power straight to You. I pray that You mold me into becoming a wife of noble character who is fearless, lacking nothing of value, and trusting in You for all things. Lord, I pray that I will be steady in my emotions and consistent in my actions to honor You and serve my husband and family well. Prepare my heart to love my husband the way that You desire me to love him, even if that means I'm sacrificing.

Proverbs 31:11-12 ESV *"The heart of her husband trusts in her, and he will have no lack of gain. She does him good, and not harm, all the days of her life."*

I pray that You bless me with supernatural wisdom that comes from You alone. Father, bless me with the words of faithfulness to encourage and uplift my husband, reminding him of who he is in You. Continue to sharpen my spiritual gifts, Lord, so that they may be used in my marriage and relationships with others. I pray that I will learn how to support my husband, uplift him, reassure him, and point him toward the cross throughout our marriage. Father, I pray that my husband will fully trust me as his best friend and wife and know that I always have his best interests at heart. Continue molding me into a prayer warrior for my future husband and household. I pray that You will teach me Your gentleness to supply comfort and love within our union.

In Jesus' name, I pray. Amen.

DECLARATIONS

Job 22:28 NKJV
*"You will decide on a matter,
and it will be established for you,
and light will shine on your ways."*

DECLARATIONS FOR YOUR FUTURE HUSBAND AND MARRIAGE

1. I declare that my husband and I will operate as one flesh, that no one can tear apart. (Matthew 19:6 ESV)

2. I declare that my husband and I will stand together and conquer, fully united in Christ. (Ecclesiastes 4:12 NLT)

3. I declare we will stand firm and courageous through trials because the Lord is with us. (Joshua 1:9 NLT)

4. I declare we will give no room to the enemy in our hearts, marriage, and family. We will not let anger divide us in Jesus' name. (Ephesians 4:27 NLT)

5. I declare we will trust You in all things and do good toward each other.(Psalm 37:3 NLT)

6. I declare we will strive for clean hearts that seek You first above all things.(Psalm 51:10 ESV)

7. I declare we will live together in unity and harmony with each other so that we may glorify Christ. (Romans 15:5–6 NLT)

8. I declare our marriage and household will be a house of prayer, worship, joy, and service. (Joshua 24:15 ESV)

9. I declare our marriage will fulfill God's purpose and plan as we submit to Christ. (Proverbs 19:21 NLT)

10. I declare in Jesus' name that our home will not be filled with fear, worry, or anxiety. We will trust in the Lord with all of our hearts. (Philippians 4:6–7 ESV)

11. I decree and declare that any evil patterns and cycles of failed and unfaithful marriages in my bloodline and in my future husband's bloodline are broken in the name of Jesus and by the blood of the Lamb. (Romans 8:2 ESV)

12. I declare Jesus Christ will be the firm foundation of our marriage.(Matthew 7:24–27 ESV)

13. I decree and declare that our marriage shall bear good fruits in Jesus' name.(Colossians 1:10 ESV)

14. I decree and declare that my husband and I will experience an overflow of blessings in our finances so that we may be a blessing to others. (Luke 6:38 ESV)

15. I decree and declare that our love and intimacy will increase as the days go by, and we will be fully satisfied with each other. (1 Corinthians 7:2–5 NLT)

16. I decree and declare God's hand is on our marriage in Jesus' name. We will leave a legacy on earth that points everyone who interacts with us to God's glory. (Psalm 112:2 NLT)

17. I decree and declare that Satan will not kill, steal, or destroy our marriage, and no weapon formed against this union shall prosper. (Isaiah 54:17 NKJV; John 10:10 NKJV)

18. I declare we will receive an abundance of blessings through our marriage.(John 10:10 NKJV)

19. I decree and declare that my husband and I will fall more and more in love with Christ as we continue to fall more and more in love with each other. (Mark 12:30 NKJV)

A MESSAGE FROM THE AUTHOR

Congratulations on completing this prayer book! It's truly inspiring to witness the transformative power of prayer. I still remember when I was first starting my journey with God - I felt uncertain about my knowledge of the Bible and my relationship with the Lord. However, my mother and family's unwavering devotion and sincere prayers supported me throughout my life. It's because of their prayers that I came to know the Lord and pursue my calling in ministry. So, believe me when I say that your prayers have the power to reach your future husband. Every prayer in this book is full of the power of the Holy Spirit, and it will have a significant impact on your life and the life of your future husband.

I feel immensely grateful for the chance to share these prayers with you. I believe that the time you are investing in praying for your future husband will create a strong foundation of faith and prayer for your life and future marriage.

Thanks for being a part of the 33 Prayers community! If you're looking for more content, don't forget to connect with me on social media and tune into The Kill Culture Podcast. I really appreciate your support and can't wait for you to see what we have in store next, including the release of our next 33 Prayers book. Thanks again for being a part of this amazing community!

Hugs and love!

Schuyler Elliot